Remembering Paris

Rebecca Schall

TURNER
PUBLISHING COMPANY

On August 25, 1944, Paris was finally liberated. Crowds of French patriots line the Champs-Elysées to view Allied tanks and trucks passing through the Arc de Triomphe. On the left, a sign states "Vive de Gaulle." At the time of liberation, Charles de Gaulle was revered as a national hero. During the war, de Gaulle created the Free French Forces. On June 18, 1940, he spoke to the French nation over the radio from London, pleading with the French to remain strong in their fight against the Germans. He proclaimed "Quoi qu'il arrive, la flame de la résistance française ne doit pas s'éteindre et ne s'éteindra pas," meaning "Whatever happens, the flame of the French Resistance must not be extinguished and will not be extinguished." This speech had a great impact on the French. De Gaulle set up intelligence networks to prevent Germans from invading England through the British Channel. The Free French Forces helped inform de Gaulle of German military activity along the Atlantic Coast and the English Channel.

Remembering Paris

Turner Publishing Company
4507 Charlotte Avenue • Suite 100
Nashville, Tennessee 37209
(615) 255-2665

Remembering Paris

www.turnerpublishing.com

Library of Congress Control Number: 2010924315

ISBN: 978-1-59652-658-7 (pbk)
ISBN: 978-1-68336-870-0 (pbk)

Printed in the United States of America

10 11 12 13 14 15 16—0 9 8 7 6 5 4 3 2

Contents

People enjoy themselves around the grand pond at the Jardin de Tuileries in 1955.

Acknowledgments

This volume, *Remembering Paris,* is the result of the cooperation and efforts of many individuals and organizations. It is with great thanks that we acknowledge the valuable contribution of the following for their generous support:

L'Agence de Roger-Viollet in Paris
The Library of Congress

For my family—Mom, Dad, and Teddy. Thank you for your uncompromising loyalty, encouragement, support, and for showing me the world.

Fran Schall
Gerry Schall
Teddy Schall
Celie Fox-Cabane
Bernard Cabane
Lyne Cohen-Solal
Mickaël Verite
Monique
Commingues
Michele Riesenmey
Nathalie Doury

Leah Boyer
Eliana McCaffery
Sergio Romero
Lee Pinkas
Kristin Henderson
Amanda Uraiqat
Pat Levin
Judson True
Andrew Lack
Mlle., M., and baby
Bronco

Preface

"If you are lucky enough to have lived in Paris as a young man, then wherever you go for the rest of your life it stays with you, for Paris is a moveable feast."

—*Ernest Hemingway*

Paris, with its magnificent architecture, historical significance, and cultural savoir faire, has the remarkable power to seduce anyone who has visited the city. Throughout the centuries, Parisians have treated their city as a masterpiece-in-progress, continually enhancing its beauty by contracting the most revered artists for its architecture, sculpture, and paintings. Parisians go to great efforts to preserve the historical and aesthetic integrity of the city, meticulously maintaining it as a piece of art in a phenomenon known in French as muséification—preserving the city as a living museum.

Located at an international crossroads where different cultures thrive, the vibrant capital is constantly changing, yet continually celebrating its historical and artistic legacy. Paris has endured everything from Viking raids to Nazi occupation, even "banalization" by invading global chain stores in recent years. For more than two millennia, the urban landscape of Paris has constantly been altered by social, political, and religious trends, as well as population growth. Each epoch has contributed something enduring to the Parisian landscape, reflecting the political demands of the people and the spirit of the age. As Paris expanded its walls to accommodate a growing population, it removed parts of its architectural heritage, while adding new layers, oftentimes incorporating the ruins of previous structures into new buildings. Today, Paris is a rich mosaic of many centuries of architecture, from preserved Gallo-Roman ruins to modern high rises.

When photography emerged in France in the nineteenth century, it allowed people to capture the modern world and document its history in an unprecedented way. Although the photographer can make decisions regarding subject matter and how to capture and present it, photographs, unlike words, seldom offer subjective interpretations of history. This lends them an authority that textual histories sometimes fail to achieve, and offers the viewer an original, untainted perspective from which to draw conclusions, interpretations, and insights.

Millions of historic photos of Paris reside in archives, both in the capital itself, and around the world. This book began with the recognition that, while those photographs are of great interest to many, they are not always easily accessible.

This book is the result of countless hours of reviewing thousands of images, in l'Agence de Roger-Viollet in Paris and the Library of Congress photographic archives, as well as extensive historical research. I greatly appreciate the generous assistance of those at Roger-Viollet and others listed in the acknowledgments, without whom this project could not have been completed.

The goal in publishing this work is to provide broader access to extraordinary photographs that will inspire, educate, and preserve Paris' past with proper respect and reverence. The photographs selected have been reproduced in their original black-and-white format. With the exception of cropping images where needed and touching up imperfections that have accrued over time, no changes have been made. The caliber and clarity of many photographs are limited by the technology of the day and the ability of the photographer at the time they were made.

This book is divided into six chapters, representing modern eras in the history of Paris. Chapter 1 looks at the city from the mid nineteenth century to 1890—one of the most pivotal times in the city's history. The period included Haussmann's rebuilding of Paris, the Prussian siege, and the Commune—the bitter civil war that followed the siege, during which Paris emerged in its modern form. The second chapter explores the period in France known as la Belle Époque, or the beautiful age, from 1890 until the eve of the First World War. Chapter 3 covers Paris from the start of the Great War through the 1920s, when Paris became a destination for the "Lost Generation." Chapter 4 looks at the turbulent interwar period of Paris in the 1930s. Chapter 5 focuses on the German occupation that Paris endured during World War II and the city's liberation by Allied forces at the war's end, and the concluding chapter takes a brief look at postwar Paris.

In each section, *Remembering Paris* attempts to capture various aspects of Parisian life through the selection of photographs, featuring important people, places, events, architecture, commerce, transportation, infrastructure, religious and educational institutions, artistic life, and everyday scenes to provide a broad perspective. I encourage readers to reflect as they gain new appreciation for the momentous history and beauty of the urban masterpiece that is Paris.

Paris is at a crossroads of land and water routes in an area rich in agriculture. This made Paris one of the leading European cities for trade, commerce, arts, learning, and culture, and a center of international transportation. This panorama of Paris was taken around 1865, during the time that Paris assumed its modern form. In the 1860s, Baron G. Haussmann annexed large tracts of land from what had once been the countryside, doubling the size of Paris to accommodate the expanding population. Twenty arrondissements, or municipal boroughs, were created in a juxtaposing clockwise circle resembling a snail's shell. More than 30 million visitors come to Paris annually, which generates the revenue needed for the preservation of old monuments, and the construction of new ones.

The New Paris—A Modern Capital

(To 1890)

Parisians stroll in the rain in 1865 on Pont au Change, a bridge connecting Île de la Cité to the Right Bank. Pont Neuf, a bridge which crosses the southern tip of Île de la Cité, is seen in the background. Pont Neuf, meaning "new bridge," is actually the oldest bridge in Paris. Construction of the bridge started in 1578 under Henri III and was completed in 1607 during the rule of Henri IV. The year 2007 marked the bridge's 400th anniversary. At the time of its construction, the bridge was ground-breaking, both for its innovative design and its beauty. Pont Neuf was built from stone to endure the centuries, while other bridges at the time, made of wood, were insubstantial and often dangerous. It was also the first bridge to be built without houses on it, allowing those on the bridge to see the river. On the banks of the Seine near Pont Neuf, traders and craftsmen had sold their goods since medieval times. Pont Neuf was also the locale for French comic theater in the seventeenth century, as well as a notorious gathering place for prostitutes, thieves, and other scoundrels. It remains a popular meeting spot today, having shed its sordid reputation.

Throughout the centuries, Parisians have continually enhanced the beauty of their city through architecture, sculpture, and paintings created by revered artists of the time. The Arc de Triomphe du Carrousel, shown here in the mid nineteenth century, sits outside the Louvre at the eastern entrance to the Tuilerie Gardens. It was built between 1806 and 1808 as a tribute to Napoleonic victories. Designed by architects Pierre-Francois Fontaine and Charles Percier and modeled after the Arch of Septimium Severus in Rome, the Arc is one of the greatest monuments of the Napoleonic era. Its regal beauty was befitting of Napoleon's Empire, with three vaults framed by columns of red and white marble, each front portraying a bas-relief of Napoleonic victories. Atop the Arc are copies of the gilded horses of St. Marco Basilica of Venice. Napoleon had the original Venetian horses removed from Italy and placed on the Arc, but he returned them in 1815, substituting exact replicas. Affectionately known by some today as the "baby Arc de Triomphe," the Arc de Triomphe du Carrousel sits in perfect alignment along the Grande Axis with the obelisk of Place de la Concorde, the larger Arc de Triomphe at Place de l'Étoile several kilometers away, and the Grand Arc de la Defense.

In this photograph from the late 1860s, people walk across Pont des Arts, the first iron bridge built in Paris. The elegant pedestrian bridge, dating from 1803, connects the Louvre on the Right Bank to the Institut de France across the Seine on the Left Bank in the 6th Arrondissement. In the background is the beautiful golden dome of the Institut de France, which was constructed as one of Cardinal Mazarin's dying wishes for a "College of the Four Nations." In 1806, Napoleon moved the Institut de France here, constituting the partnership of the Sciences, Letters, Fine Arts, and Moral and Political Sciences. One part of the Institut is the Académie Française, where "immortals," who are elected for life, act as the guardians of the French language, safeguarding its purity from foreign influences and Anglicization.

Pictured here in this mid-nineteenth-century photograph is the Tour Saint Jacques, the St. Jacques Tower, in the 4th Arrondissement. The striking Gothic monument, standing at 170 feet, is the only remaining part of an old Renaissance church, Saint-Jacques-la-Boucherie, dedicated to Saint James during the reign of François I in the early sixteenth century. *Boucherie,* meaning "butcher," is part of the church's name because it was patronized mostly by wealthy butchers from the nearby market, Les Halles. Blaise Pascal, the seventeenth-century French scientist and philosopher, used the tower to perform barometrical experiments. A statue of him now stands at ground level. The church was destroyed in 1797, but the tower remained intact, inspiring Alexandre Dumas, author of *The Three Musketeers,* to write the 1856 play *La Tour Saint-Jacques-la-Boucherie.* The tower has been covered in scaffolding in recent years for renovation, and Parisians await its unveiling.

Place du Châtelet, pictured here in the mid nineteenth century, is a public square on the Right Bank, dating from 1808. Its sphinx fountains celebrate Napoleon's successful Egyptian campaign and his other triumphs. Tour Saint Jacques can be seen in the background.

Place St. Germain l'Auxerrois, shown here in the mid nineteenth century at 2 Place du Louvre in the 1st Arrondissement in the center of Paris, is also known as the Church of the Louvre. It was founded in the seventh century and has been rebuilt many times over the centuries. French kings, when they still lived at the Louvre, attended mass here. Its bell, named "Marie," rang on August 24, 1572, marking the massacres of St. Bartholomew's Day, when thousands of French Protestants, in Paris for the wedding of Henri IV of Navarre and Margot of Valois, were massacred by zealot Catholics and French soldiers during the Wars of Religion.

People have been passing through the Paris area for thousands of years. In 250 B.C., a Celtic subtribe known as the Parisii set up permanent settlements around the Seine. It is from this tribe that the name Paris is derived. Caesar conquered Paris in 52 B.C. as part of his western campaigns, and turned the small Celtic fishing village into a European city. The Romans subsequently built a settlement known as Lutetia, or Lutèce, on the Left Bank and on Île de la Cité. Lutèce became a wealthy outpost of the Roman Empire, with impressive temples, palaces, bathhouses, an amphitheater, and a forum. Palais des Thermes, or the Thermes de Cluny, shown here in the mid nineteenth century, is the remains of a third-century Gallo-Roman bathhouse located in the 5th Arrondissement, just blocks from the Sorbonne to the south, and near the Seine to the north. The baths were public, part of the ancient Roman effort to civilize the ancient Parisii. The ruins have been incorporated into the Musée des Môyen-Ages, the museum of the Middle Ages. The Thermes, along with the Arènes de Lutèce, are the only standing remains from Gallo-Roman Paris.

In 1871, the prolonged strain of food shortages, Prussian bombardment, and military disaster, compounded by the discontent of workers and the poorer classes, contributed to the start of the civil war in Paris known as the Commune. During the Siege of Paris and the Commune, more damage was done to the capital than in any other conflict in its history. French treasures, monuments, and governmental and administrative buildings were incinerated. The ruins on rue de Lille in the 7th Arrondissement, pictured here in 1871, show some of the Commune damage.

Boulevard St. Denis, shown here in the mid to late nineteenth century, is one of the oldest streets in Paris. French kings took this road before entering Paris, and the boulevard led to the burial place of the kings at the Church of Saint Denis. Louis XIV had the gate in this picture built in 1672, replacing the medieval city gate. At the time, the gate was outside Paris city limits. The boulevard has always been a lively area, and today is still a busy market neighborhood known for its fashion warehouses and ethnic cuisine.

The legendary head of the Statue of Liberty, destined for New York, was on display in a park in Paris in 1883. Before that, her head was presented at the Paris Exposition in 1879 in the Trocadero Palace Garden. The statue, dedicated in 1886 and officially named *Liberty Enlightening the World (La Liberté éclairant le monde),* was a gift from France to the United States to commemorate the centennial anniversary of the Declaration of Independence, a gesture of friendship between sister republics. Auguste Bartholdi designed the famous lady, and she was internally engineered by Gustave Eiffel, the man who designed the Eiffel Tower. Various charities, fund-raisers, and donations raised the necessary $250,000 for construction. Today, the American icon stands watch in New York harbor, welcoming all who come to the United States of America.

Hôtel de Ville, shown here in 1884 from the quai of the Right Bank of the Seine, stands on the site where public executions took place for half a millennium. It was inside the original Hôtel de Ville, built in the sixteenth century, that Revolutionary leader Maximilien Robespierre closed himself off with his cohorts, away from the soldiers of the Convention on July 27, 1794. When the leaders of the Convention burst into the building, Robespierre shot off half his own jaw with a pistol in a botched suicide attempt. Robespierre was taken to the Conciergerie to be killed the next day at the guillotine to which he himself had sent thousands. The original Hôtel de Ville was destroyed by fire during the Paris Commune of 1871. The building that now stands was designed by famous architects Deperthes and Ballu and was completed in 1882 in the same style as the original building. It is now the municipal headquarters of Paris.

Paris has always been a city of artistic achievement. A group of art students in Paris pose in 1885 at Academie Julian, a private art school established in 1860. The state art school, École des Beaux-Arts, prohibited women from enrolling because it was considered improper for them to have the same training as men, especially in nude portraiture, but Academie Julian welcomed women to enroll. It was popular with Americans as well. Eventually, it expanded to other campuses around Paris and merged with the École Supérieure d'Arts Graphiques in 1968.

The Eiffel Tower, the icon that most people envision when they think of Paris, is shown here on July 19, 1888, during the middle stages of its construction. The iron tower was designed by Gustave Eiffel and built by co-architects Emile Naugier, Maurice Koechlin, and Steven Sauvestre for the 1889 Exposition Universelle on Champs de Mars on the Left Bank of the Seine. It is hard to imagine a Paris without the Eiffel Tower, but its construction in Paris was a turn of fate. Gustave Eiffel intended to build the Eiffel Tower in Spain for the Universal Exposition of Barcelona in 1888, but his designs were rejected.

Gustave Eiffel and four others pose in 1888 beside a staircase on the summit of the Eiffel Tower. Intended to be a temporary structure easy to raze, it had only a twenty-year permit. City officials, however, began to recognize the tower's great value for communication. During World War I, it was used for radio transmission, and Parisian taxis left there to take soldiers to the front lines in the First Battle of the Marne. During the German occupation of Paris in World War II, the Eiffel Tower was used to broadcast German television to injured German soldiers in local hospitals. The tower's role in radio and television communications continues today.

This image of the Eiffel Tower hydraulic machinery, taken during the Paris Exposition of 1889, shows a man beside the wheel that raises the elevator up the tower. The Eiffel Tower remained the tallest structure in the world until 1930, when Manhattan's Chrysler Building won the title. Today, with a new antenna, the Eiffel Tower stands 1,063 feet tall and weighs more than 7,300 tons. It also has two restaurants, Altitude 95 and Jules Verne, a very expensive eatery with its own elevator.

The Pavilion of Venetian Glassmaking near the foot of the Eiffel Tower was one of the numerous European exhibits participating in the Exposition Universelle of 1889.

Pictured here through the base of the Eiffel Tower is the Gas Pavilion, one of 80 structures built on the Champs de Mars during the Paris Exposition Universelle of 1889. The series of Universal Expositions held in Paris in the late nineteenth century punctuated stages of the rebirth and development of the city. Each exposition debuted exciting technological advances that would revolutionize the way people lived their lives.

This 1889 photograph shows the interior of the 1,452-foot Gallery of Machines (Palais des Machines) built by Ferdinand Dutert, with machines being set up for presentation at the Exposition Universelle of 1889.

Pedestrians traverse the Passerelle de l'Alma, an ornate footbridge on the Quai d'Orsay, constructed during the Paris Universal Exposition of 1889.

Large pieces of ice float in the Seine during the harsh winter of 1890–1891, which is making it difficult for boats such as the *Figaro,* pictured here, to transport people and goods on the river. In the background is Pont Neuf. Parisian winters today are usually less severe.

The Pont au Change Bridge and the Palais du Justice behind it are pictured here in the late nineteenth century. Pont au Change, so named for the goldsmiths and change vendors who once worked on the bridge, connects the Palace of Justice on Île de la Cité to the Right Bank. On the right side is La Conciergerie, built as a palace at the end of the thirteenth century under Philip the Fair. It was a prison from the sixteenth century onward; most notably, it served as the detention point for thousands of French citizens considered enemies of the French Revolution in the late eighteenth century. They spent their last days in the medieval prison cells before being carted to their beheadings at the guillotine in Place de la Revolution across the Seinc. Marie Antoinette, the most famous inmate, was imprisoned here from August 2 until October 16, 1793, when she went to her death nine months after her husband, Louis XVI, the King of France, lost his head. One can visit the Conciergerie and walk in the footsteps of the condemned being led to the guillotine.

The Pantheon and rue Soufflot are seen here in the late nineteenth century. Upon recovering from a serious illness, King Louis XV had the Pantheon built as a church dedicated to St. Genevieve. Architect Jacques-German Soufflot designed the Pantheon of Paris in neoclassical style, modeled after the Roman Pantheon. Construction began in 1758, but the Pantheon was not completed until 1789 at the start of the French Revolution. Because the Revolution outlawed religion, it was turned into a mausoleum for the great men of France *(les Grands Hommes),* including Voltaire, Victor Hugo, Rousseau, Emile Zola, as well as Marie-Curie, the first woman laid to rest in the Pantheon.

With the coming of the railway, an unparalleled number of provincial migrants flooded Paris, attracted by new jobs created by the Industrial Revolution. Shown here is the Gare du Nord in the 1890s. The train station, built in 1864, displays allegorical figures on its facade representing towns that the station's trains serve in northern France and the rest of Europe. The introduction of the train in the nineteenth century fundamentally changed the way people worked and lived. It enabled workers to migrate to cities, providing labor during the Industrial Revolution and accelerating urbanization. It also allowed people to escape the city on weekends and explore the rest of France and Europe, signifying the birth of modern tourism. Today, Gare du Nord is an international train station. Travelers can take the Eurostar high speed train from here, ride beneath the British Channel through what is commonly referred to as the Chunnel, and arrive in London in little more than two hours.

La Belle Époque—The Beautiful Age

(1891–1914)

The fountain at the Luxembourg Gardens in the 6th Arrondissement froze during the infamously bitter winter of 1893. The Jardin de Luxembourg, at 224,500 square meters, is Paris' largest park. The Luxembourg Palace at the north end of the garden was built for Marie de' Medici in the early seventeenth century by architect Salomon de Brosse in the style of a Florentine villa to appease the homesick Italian Queen. The palace now houses the French Senate. The garden is always packed with people, who sit for hours reading on chairs around the fountain or having picnics, and children who play with toy boats in the fountain. In Victor Hugo's *Les Miserables,* Luxembourg Gardens is where Cosette and Jean Valjean meet Marius.

Observers examine the aftermath of a freak train accident at Gare Montparnasse on October 22, 1895. The Granville-Paris Express derailed when it exceeded a buffer stop, crashing through the two-foot-thick wall of the train station and plummeting to the ground 30 feet below at Place des Rennes. There were no casualties among the train passengers, but falling debris killed a woman on the street.

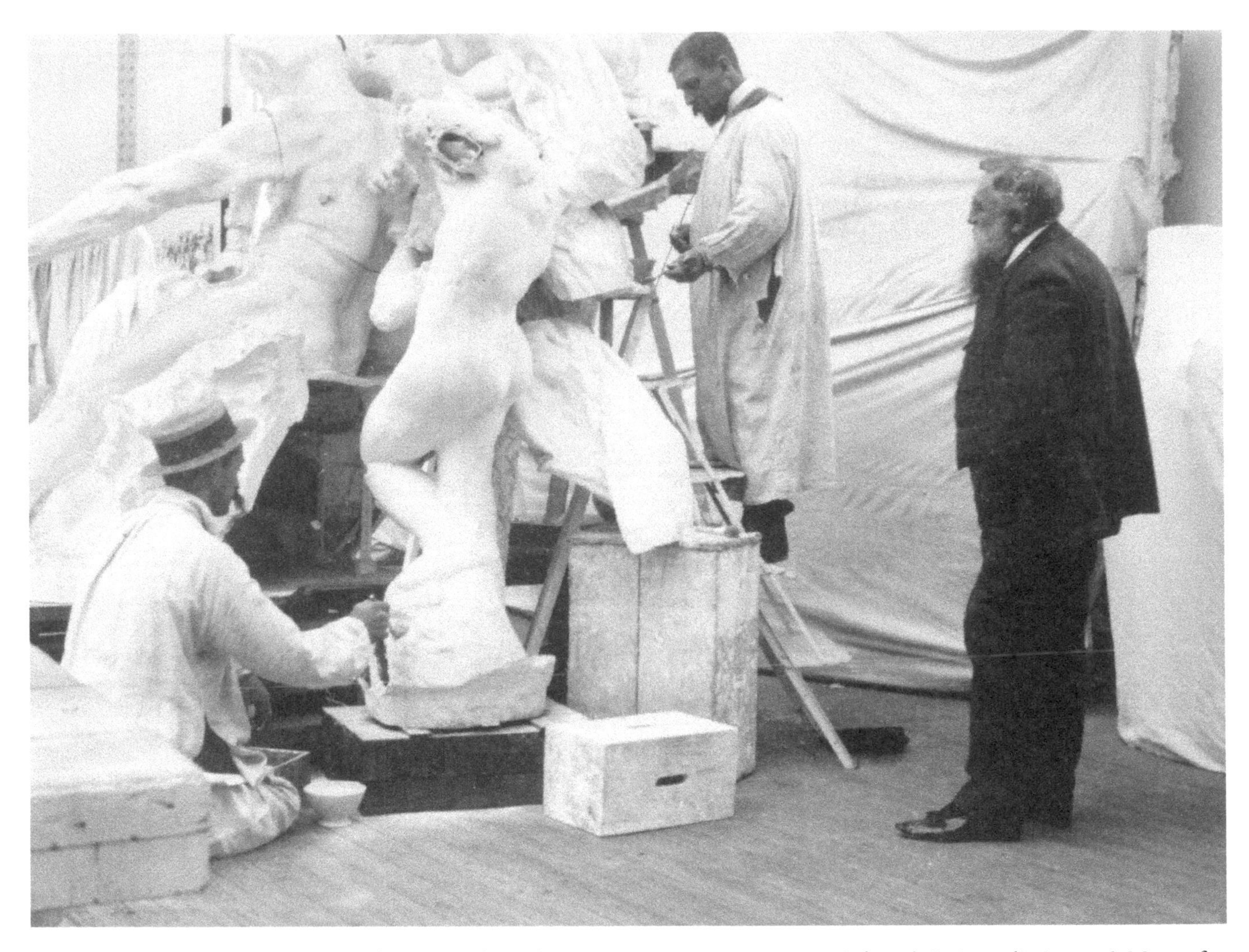

The French sculptor Auguste Rodin observes work on the monument to Victor Hugo at Lebossé's Paris studio in 1896. Many of Rodin's works, including *The Thinker, The Gates of Hell,* and *The Burghers of Calais,* are on display at the Rodin Museum in Paris.

French political figure, journalist, and novelist Emile Zola sits in the garden of his home in Verneuil-sur-Seine with his friend Jeanne Rozerot and their two children, Denise and Jacques. Zola chronicled important developments in French society in the latter half of the nineteenth century in his novels. He took a bold career move when he published "J'accuse" on the front page of *L'Aurore* as an open letter to President Félix Faure on January 13, 1898, which accused the French government and military of flagrant anti-Semitism for the wrongful arrest and conviction of Alfred Dreyfus. His letter was hugely influential in exposing Dreyfus' unjust treatment. Zola himself had been tried for libel in the affair in 1899 and convicted the following year, resulting in his removal from the Legion of Honor, and he fled to England to escape imprisonment, although he was later pardoned. Zola died on September 29, 1902, at the age of 62 of carbon monoxide poisoning from a closed chimney pipe in his house—a suspicious death believed to be politically motivated foul play. Zola is buried in the Pantheon among others significant to French history.

This garden scene was photographed around 1900 at the Moulin Rouge. The iconic cabaret was built in 1889 by Joseph Oller on Boulevard de Clichy, near Montmartre in the notorious red light district of Pigalle in the 18th Arrondissement. Cancan dancers once performed on the stage while the orchestra played from inside the giant stucco elephant. Paris at this time had earned an international reputation as a city of sin, with its many cabarets, brothels, and dance halls. After Paris' rapid and devastating defeat to the Prussians in 1870, the egos of Parisians were bruised, and cabarets, fêtes, world's fairs, and mass culture and entertainments were cultivated in the following decades in an effort to heal France's wounded spirit and move toward an idealized future. This, in turn, helped forge a common identity and shared Parisian culture within the modernizing metropolis. The Moulin Rouge, which for many symbolizes the carefree romanticism of the Belle Époque, remains today a popular tourist destination.

This photograph was taken during the Belle Époque in a room of Roman art at the Hôtel de Cluny, the medieval history museum of Paris. Hôtel de Cluny is one of the best preserved examples of medieval architecture in Paris. Built in 1334, and rebuilt in the late fifteenth century, it used to be a townhouse for the abbots of Cluny. Mary Tudor lived here in 1515 after the death of her husband, Louis XII of France, so that Francis I could observe her for signs of pregnancy with the heir to the French throne. Cardinal Mazarin also lived here for a time. In 1833, Alexandre Sommerand moved to the Hôtel de Cluny, bringing his vast collection of medieval and Renaissance art and artifacts. After his death in 1842, the French state purchased his collection, and the Hôtel de Cluny reopened as a museum. The most famous work in the museum today is the series of six late-fifteenth-century Flemish tapestries known as *The Lady and the Unicorn (La Dame à la Licorne),* seen as one of the greatest works of medieval European art.

This postcard from around 1900 shows a panorama of Gare d'Orsay, the train station newly built for the Universal Exposition of 1900. During World War II, it was used as a mailing center. In 1977, work began to convert the station to a museum, which finally opened its doors on December 1, 1986, inaugurated by French President Francois Mitterrand. Musee d'Orsay showcases French art from 1848–1914 and is revered for its Impressionist masterpieces by artists such as Claude Monet and Pierre-Auguste Renoir, which influenced later art movements like Neo-Impressionism, Post-Impressionism, cubism, and fauvism. Also showcased are works by artists including Vincent Van Gogh, Edgar Degas, Gustave Courbet, Auguste Rodin, Paul Gaugin, Paul Cézanne, Édouard Manet, Georges Seurat, and Henri de Toulouse-Lautrec among many other artists, most of whom were considered radicals in their time for their departure from academic painting styles.

This photograph was taken after a wedding at Saint-Etienne-du-Mont on May 2, 1900. Well-dressed gentlemen and ladies with parasols stroll across the square near this extraordinary church located next to the Pantheon in the 5th Arrondissement. The church, with its unusual facade, combines French Renaissance and Gothic elements. Its architecturally innovative interior contains some of Paris' best preserved Renaissance stained-glass windows, as well as the remains of St. Geneviève, the patron saint of Paris who saved the city from the Huns in the year 451. Blaise Pascal and Jean Racine are also entombed here.

Two women await treatment for their dogs at the Society for Animal Relief, a free Parisian clinic, in the late nineteenth century. Anyone who has been to Paris has likely observed the love, or in some cases, obsession, that Parisians have for their dogs. Parisians ride with their dogs on the Metro, take them into stores, and dine with them in cafes and restaurants.

This 1900s postcard shows Place des Vosges, Paris' oldest and according to many, most beautiful square, located in the 3rd Arrondissement in the Marais district. Built between 1605 and 1612 by King Henri IV as the first of many programs to beautify the capital, the square was originally known as Place Royale. King Henri II was mortally wounded in a jousting tournament here in 1559. The perfectly symmetrical square is 140 meters by 140 meters (455 feet by 455 feet), with nine uniform houses built on each side on the designs of Baptiste du Cerceaw. The distinctive red-brick design of the 36 buildings with stone strips over porticoes and vaulted arches complements the lush trees, manicured gardens, and fountain in the center of the square. A bronze statue of Louis XIII once stood in the center of the square but was melted down during the Revolution. A replica of the original was erected in 1825. The square was renamed Place des Vosges in 1800 after the *département* of the Vosges, which paid taxes for a campaign of the Revolutionary army. Facing each other on the south and north sides of Place des Vosges are the luxurious Pavilion of the King and the ornate Pavilion of the Queen, although no royalty lived there. There have been many famous inhabitants of the square, including Cardinal Richelieu, Madame de Sevigné, and Victor Hugo, who wrote much of *Les Miserables* while living in Place des Vosges. Today, art galleries, fashionable restaurants, and musicians occupy the buildings of Place des Vosges.

The Eiffel Tower and the globe from Point Passay built for the Exposition Universelle in 1900 are shown here. The exposition, the fifth World's Fair held in Paris in less than half a century, was the grandest yet, with more than 50 million in attendance from April to November, setting a new world's record. The new Art Nouveau style of the age permeated all aspects of the fair. Many innovations of the day were debuted, including talking films, the escalator, and the diesel engine, which ran on peanut oil. Campbell's Soup was awarded a gold medal, which remains on the company's labels today. Many of Paris' most famous landmarks were built for this fair, including the Grand Palais and Petit Palais, Pont Alexandre III, Gare d'Orsay (now Musée d'Orsay), Gare d'Orleans, and the Paris Metro. Paris was also host to the Second Olympic Games in 1900.

Prince Charles Louis de Bourbon and Monsieur Tourrand stand in front of the steam omnibus of the "Société Anonyme des Générateurs Economique" of Paris in the early 1900s. The prince had Legitimist claims to the Bourbon crown of France as Charles XI after his father died in 1887, and he was also the Carlist claimant to the Spanish throne as Carlos VII, Duke of Madrid, after his father abdicated the Spanish throne in 1868.

Shown here in 1900 is a woman selling floral bouquets at the Flower Market of Paris on Île de la Cité. Scenes of women selling flowers at the market were painted by many French artists of the day.

This photograph focuses on the back side of Notre Dame, with its famous flying buttresses shooting out toward the Seine. Construction began on Notre Dame Cathedral on Île de la Cité, one of two islands in Paris in the middle of the Seine, in 1193 under Bishop Maurice de Sully and was completed in 1345. Over the past eight centuries, it has undergone many incarnations and alterations. During the French Revolution, when many churches and religious objects were destroyed, Notre Dame was saved and used as a "Temple of Reason" by Revolutionary leader Maximilien Robespierre. Resanctified in 1802, this cathedral is where Napoleon crowned himself Holy Roman Emperor in 1804 as Pope Pius VII looked on.

Notre Dame Cathedral, shown here in 1901, was a turning point in Gothic architecture at the time of its construction. It was built with six-partite vaulting, five aisles, and a three portal facade, making the cathedral a massive building to receive worshipers. It is vertically separated into thirds by pilasters, and both vertically and horizontally by galleries. Its famous rose window, measuring 33 feet in diameter, dates from 1220–1225, with an eighteenth-century organ beneath it. The massive cathedral is nearly 500 feet long, 164 feet wide, and 115 feet tall, and can accommodate 9,000 people. It is lined with small chapels filled with seventeenth-century art. Victor Hugo's *Hunchback of Notre Dame* told of Quasimodo, the hunchback who guarded the cathedral and had an impossible love for Esmeralda, the beautiful Gypsy dancer. Before his novel came out, authorities considered demolishing the decaying cathedral. Hugo's novel, published in 1831, inspired the public to demand that Notre Dame be saved and renovated, which eventually was undertaken by Eugene Viollet-le-Duc, between 1844 and 1864.

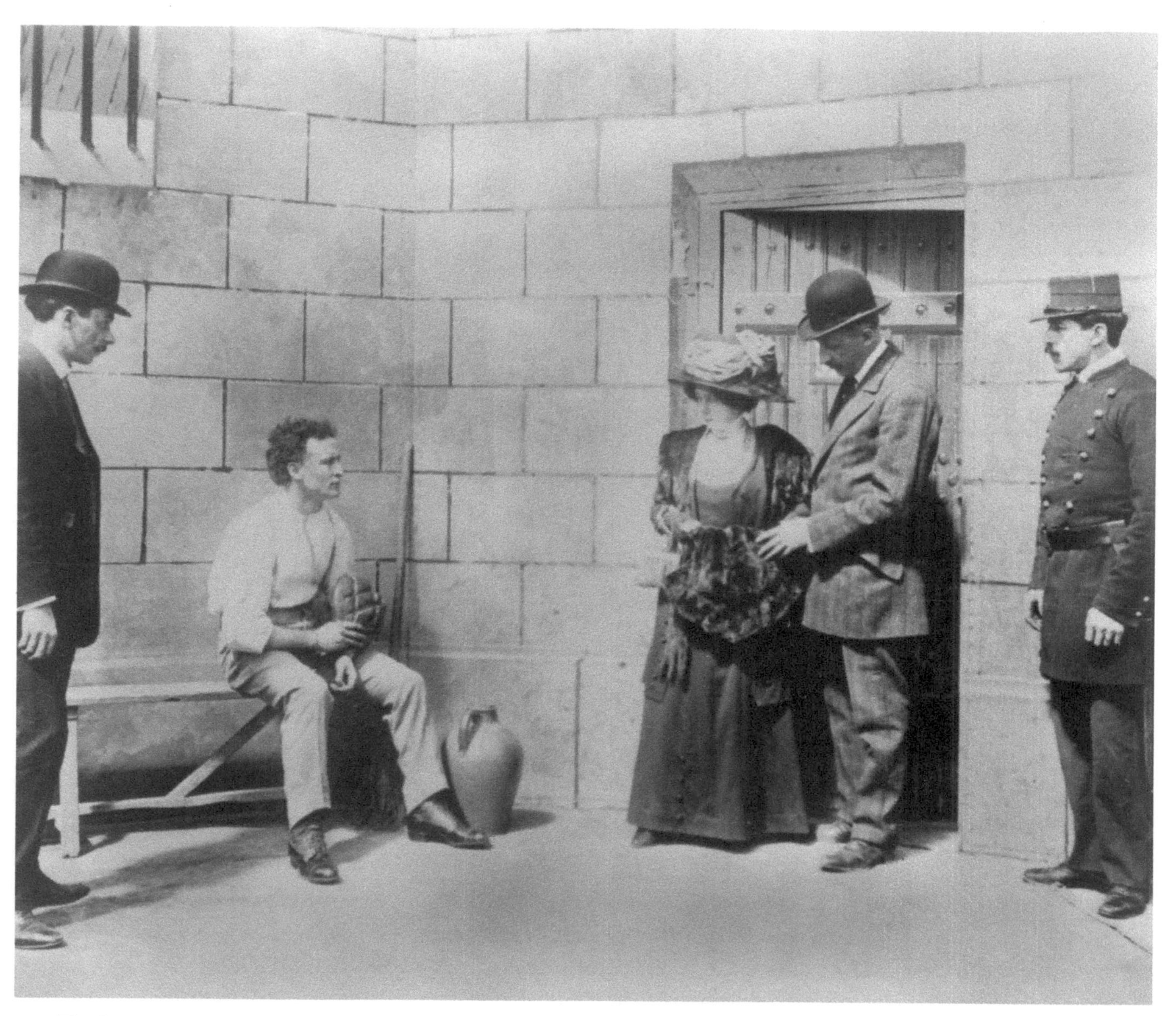

The famous magician, stunt artist, and "escapologist" Harry Houdini (1874–1926), known as the "Handcuff King," performs a prison break in a short film produced in 1901 in Paris by Pathe Frères, the record and film production company founded by brothers Charles, Emile, Jacques, and Théophile Pathe.

Shown here is the Gallery d'Apollon in the Louvre in 1901. In the sixteenth century, when the Louvre was still a royal palace, King Francis I began amassing an art collection which continued to be enlarged by successive kings. The Louvre was used to exhibit art under Louis XIV, and on August 10, 1793, the Louvre opened as a museum for the general public. The already huge art collection was greatly enhanced by Napoleon I, who claimed great works of art and national treasures as conquests of war from the countries he invaded. Much of the art in the Louvre today originated from Napoleon's spoils of war in the early nineteenth century. Today, the Louvre houses more than 400,000 pieces, ranging from ancient art to mid-nineteenth-century European, Asian, and African art. Among these are some of the most famous works of art in the world, such as the *Venus de Milo,* the *Nike of Samothrace,* the *Mona Lisa (La Jaconde),* David's *Coronation of Napoleon,* Gericault's *Raft of the Medusa,* and Delacroix' *Liberty Leading the People.* Napoleon constructed a northern wing to the Louvre, which was completed during the reign of his nephew, Napoleon III.

Avenue du Bois and the Arc de Triomphe on a day in 1903. One of Paris' most celebrated landmarks, the Arc de Triomphe was commissioned by Napoleon after his victory at Austerlitz in 1806, although the Arc was not completed until 1836 under King Louis-Philippe during the July Monarchy. Architect Jean Chalgrin modeled its neoclassical design on ancient Roman monuments to befit his army and use as the centerpiece to display military victories in triumphant marches.

The Champs-Elysées, looking toward Place de la Concorde, is busily traversed here in 1903. This elegant boulevard is more than a mile long in the 8th Arrondissement of Paris, spanning from the Arc de Triomphe in the west to the Place de la Concorde in the east. Once an area of swamps and then hunting fields and market gardens, today the Champs-Elysées is an upscale shopping avenue and Europe's most expensive real estate. It is known as "la plus belle avenue du monde" (the most beautiful avenue in the world). It is the site of famous and infamous military marches, Bastille Day celebrations, and the ending point of the Tour de France bicycle race.

Construction of the Metro, pictured here in July 1906 at Place Saint-Michel on rue Danton in the 6th Arrondissement, resembles a whale skeleton. The Paris Metro was built in Art Nouveau style for the Exposition Universelle of 1900. Today, its 133 miles of routes are covered by 16 lines, and are used by 4.5 million people daily. In the back center of this photograph is Fountain Saint Michel, with its pink marble columns, two on each side of the marble statue of Saint Michel slaying the dragon. The fountain has been a popular meeting spot since it was built in 1860, and droves of people are always assembled in front of it. Sometimes, mischievous students put soap into the fountain, turning it into a massive bubble bath.

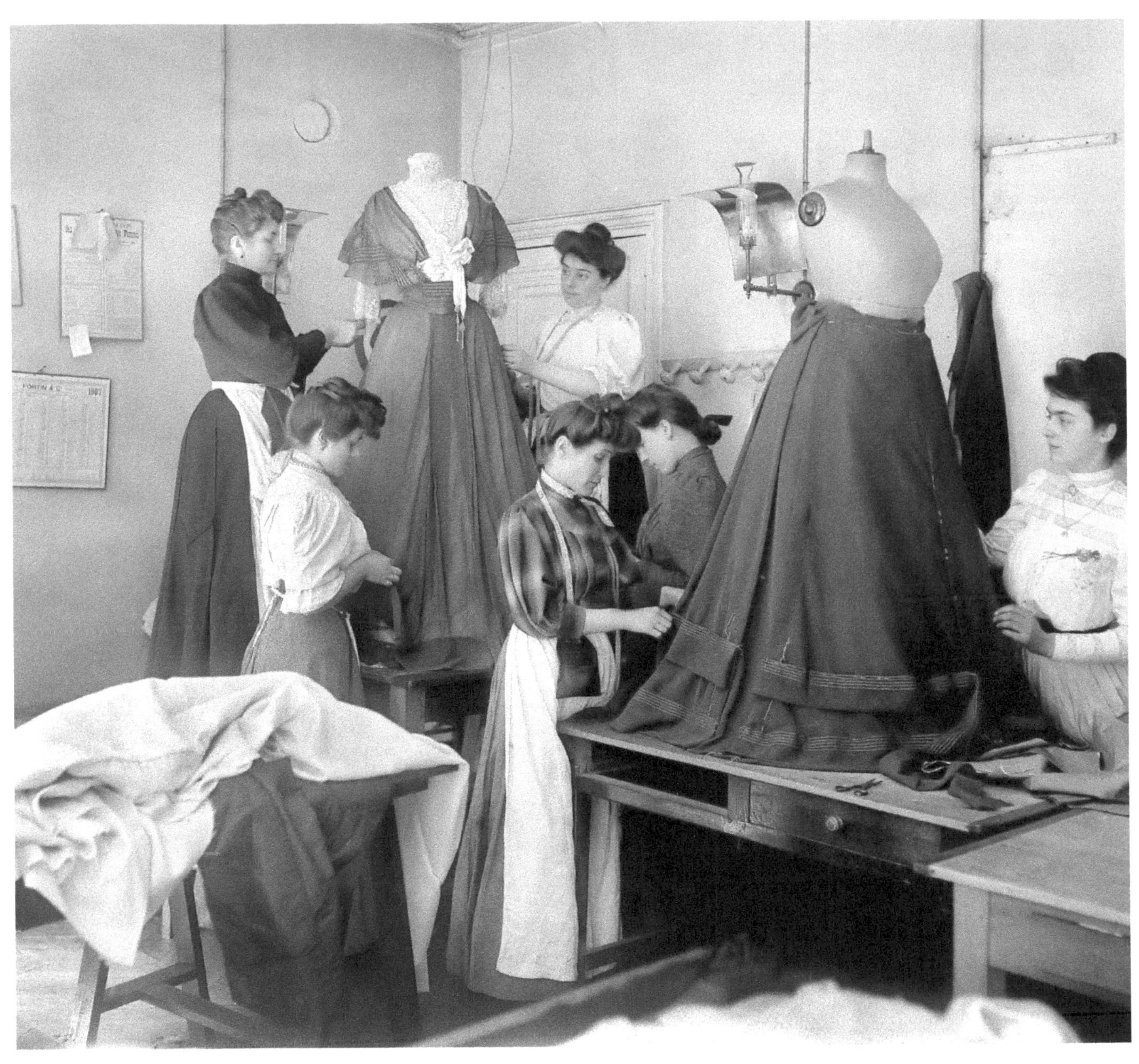

Paris has long been reputed for high fashion. Pictured here in 1907, women work to create chic dresses for wealthy clientele in one of the grand design houses in Paris.

Fascinated Parisians look at the Diplodocus, a Jurassic-era dinosaur at an exhibition at the Natural History Museum in Jardin de Plantes in the 5th Arrondissement. This fossilized skeleton, discovered in Wyoming in 1887, was presented to France as a gift from the United States. This particular genus, the *D. Carnegiei,* is the most famous kind of diplodocus, and casts of it are displayed all over the world. The museum exhibit was inaugurated by French president Fallières on June 15, 1908. At this time, the discovery of dinosaurs was recent. Most people had never seen a dinosaur skeleton and viewed these seemingly fantastical beasts with amazement and disbelief.

The Eiffel Tower and surrounding grounds mark the year 1909 in this view facing the Seine and the Trocadéro Palace. The Trocadéro was named for the Battle of Trocadéro in Southern Spain in 1823, when French forces defeated rebels and restored Spanish Bourbon rule to the throne. The Trocadéro Palace was built for the 1878 Exposition Universelle as a meeting place for various organizations, but it was razed and replaced with the Chaillot Palace for the 1937 Exposition Universelle.

Shown here in 1910 is a woman selling massive pumpkins at Les Halles, the wholesale food market of Paris located since medieval times in the 1st Arrondissement on the Right Bank. Emile Zola wrote about Les Halles in his novel *Le Ventre de Paris,* calling the market "the belly of Paris." The historic market was demolished in 1971 to the sorrow of many Parisians, and the wholesale market moved to the suburbs. The former Les Halles is now an expansive underground shopping complex.

The grand staircase of the Opera Garnier is shown here in 1901. The interior is as extravagantly designed as the exterior of the building. An 1877 painting of this staircase by French artist Louis Beroud hangs in the Carnavalet Museum in Paris. Nazi bombs fell through the ceiling of the Opera during World War II, and the damage on the stairs can still be seen. Marc Chagall paintings completed in 1966 adorn the hall and ceiling. Underground water discovered at the site of the Opera slowed construction, and inspired Gaston Leroux in his novel *Phantom of the Opera,* about a phantom that lived on the lake beneath the Opera who tutored and fell in love with the young ballet dancer and opera singer, Christine.

The exterior of Opera Garnier, the most well known building of the era of Napoleon III, is shown here in the early 1900s at the crossroads of Haussmann's grand new boulevards. This Second Empire neo-Baroque masterpiece was designed and built between 1862 and 1875 by Charles Garnier, who was selected over 171 other architects. The opulence of the Second Empire is exemplified in the Opera's many marble pillars and sculptures, and extravagant display of gold. It is the world's largest opera venue, with an interior of 120,000 square feet and a stage that can hold 450 performers. A statue of Apollo, the ancient Greco-Roman god of music, crowns the top of the Opera.

Two workers in a rowboat are surveying the high-water levels in the Montparnasse Metro station, inundated during the famous Paris floods in January 1910. Floods are natural centennial occurrences in Paris, but the winter of 1910 saw the worst flooding in the city's history following heavy rainstorms. The waters crested the tenth day, and took more than a month to subside. On January 28, floodwaters rose to more than 27 feet in some parts of Paris. The floods closed down the Metro from January through April 1910, less than a decade after the first Metro train went into service. Floods threatened the countless works of precious art stored around Paris in underground vaults, and many of these works had to be evacuated.

Parisians continued on with their lives as best they could during the flood of 1910. People traveled around the city by boat, or as shown here on Avenue Ledru-Rollin, they crossed streets carefully on elevated planks. Other areas around Paris also suffered severe damage owing to the interconnection of local hydraulic systems. Damage from the floods, in modern currency, exceeded tens of billions of dollars. Although the Seine is better controlled these days by a computer system and by four dams, another destructive flood is quite possible.

La Madeleine, pictured here in 1911, is one of the legacies of Napoleon. Modeled on a Greek temple, it was built by the architect Vignon between 1806 and 1814 to honor Napoleon's army. Situated on the site of a former medieval synagogue at the end of rue Royale in Place St. Mary Magdalene, La Madeleine is dedicated to the same saint. The 65-foot-tall church has 52 Corinthian columns and a prominently displayed frieze created by master sculptor Lemaire in 1834 depicting the Last Judgment.

Since the seventeenth century, booksellers known as *les bouquinistes* have sold used books and art on the quais of the Seine, as shown in this picture from December 1913. Originally, these booksellers had to push carts to sell their books, but since the time of Napoleon III, permanent green stalls have existed on the quais. The bouquinistes still sell used and rare books, antiques, posters, paintings, souvenirs, and various oddities from stalls on both sides of the Seine.

The entrance to a Paris Metro station is guarded by French infantry in August 1914. Dreading another German occupation, the French government relocated to Bordeaux at the start of the war. Because of German follies, poor implementation, bad maneuvering on the part of the Germans, French fortitude in defending their own lines, and an Allied victory in 1914 at the First Battle of the Marne, Paris evaded occupation. During the battle, German troops had advanced to a mere 15 miles from Paris. When the French government chartered a thousand Parisian taxis to take French soldiers to the front lines, an event known as the "Miracle on the Marne," the Germans were pushed back 75 miles, to the Oise.

Hundreds of French reservists gather outside Gare de l'Est, the station where many French troops mobilized during World War I and where injured troops returned before being taken to French hospitals.

French reservists are headed to Gare de l'Est in 1914, where they will embark for the war. Gare de l'Est, one of Paris' oldest and largest train stations, opened in 1849. Queen Victoria arrived there for the Exposition Universelle in 1855 and was met at the station by Napoleon III. Atop the station is a statue representing Strasbourg, because trains from Gare de l'Est head east toward that city. The station is still the Paris terminus for the Orient Express, which began its service to Istanbul in 1883.

French colonial troops, such as the Senegalese tirailleurs, pictured here heading off to war in 1914, were an integral part of the war effort, yet they were treated poorly when they returned to their native countries. Many of them and their children eventually joined groups that would play a key role in the French political crisis of decolonization after World War II.

With the start of World War I, hundreds of Americans volunteered to fight for France, as shown here in August 1914, although at this point the United States had not yet officially joined the war. America had a policy of neutrality until Germany declared unrestricted submarine warfare in 1917. When President Wilson decided to bring the United States into the war, he called it a quest to make the world "safe for democracy."

Troops march through the courtyard of Les Invalides, while a man who lost his legs in the war is carried through the street by soldiers. Men with missing limbs were common sights in Paris during and after the war.

Onlookers gaze at a French regiment about to leave for the front lines at Place de la Concorde in December 1915.

The Great War and the Golden Twenties

(1915–1929)

Not yet in uniform or aware of what awaits them on the frontlines of battle, young soldiers prepare to go to Montparnasse train station en route to the war in January 1916.

Soldiers depart for war at Gare Montparnasse in January 1916. A young man at center is wearing a sign warning people to be silent and not trust anyone, because the ears of the enemy are listening.

Pictured here is an unexploded zeppelin in a factory at 100 rue de Ménilmontant in the 20th Arrondissement on January 29, 1916. Paris was also fired upon during World War I by Big Bertha, a World War I L/14 heavy mortar Howitzer whose 820-kilogram shells could travel nearly eight miles. Big Bertha had a fearsome reputation, and Germans intended to use it to destroy Northern French and Belgian forts, which it did effectively for a while, but it failed to destroy France's new steel-reinforced concrete fort at Verdun.

French children watch as American soldiers draw 1545KK guns into firing position at a tractor and artillery school in St. Naur, Paris, on May 9, 1918. Scarcely more than two decades later, many French boys who lived through World War I, the "war to end all wars," would be called on to fight for France in World War II. In 1918, the Spanish influenza spread throughout Paris, and the rest of Europe. People already weakened by hunger and the war, especially children and the elderly, were particularly susceptible. This virulent strain, similar to that of the bird flu today, killed 50 million people worldwide, five times that of World War I itself.

Frenchwomen in 1919 tediously repair the carpets at Versailles in the magnificent Hall of Mirrors, where the Treaty of Versailles finally would be signed. Versailles had once been the seat of royal power under Louis XIV. Louis XIV, also known as the Sun King, ruled by divine right and absolute power, and raised France to be the most powerful nation in the world during the seventeenth century, known as "le Grand Siècle," or the Great Century. He was the most extravagant and opulent European monarch since the days of the Roman Empire, and the lavish palace he built at Versailles is a testament to that power. Because of his extravagance and excess and the constant wars he waged with neighboring countries financed through the taxation of French peasantry, the monarchy entered decline, the country found itself in financial ruin, and the seeds of revolution were planted.

Following the signing of the Treaty of Versailles in 1919, French prime minister Georges Clemenceau (at left, lifting his hat), American president Woodrow Wilson, and British prime minister David Lloyd George (at right) pose for a photograph. Clemenceau, nicknamed "the Tiger," was actively involved throughout the negotiations leading to the Treaty of Versailles. Germany was kept out of the negotiations, and at first refused the terms of the treaty. On June 20, however, the new German chancellor, Gustav Bauer, agreed to the terms, to the infuriation of many Germans, who saw it as a betrayal. The Treaty of Versailles instilled much of the resentment and desire for revenge that was used as a selling point by Nazis and other extremist groups in the years to come.

Clemenceau personally decided that the treaty ending World War I should be signed in the Hall of Mirrors, which symbolized the essence of French power during the reign of Louis XIV, the Sun King. This grand room was also the site where Prussian King William I was declared Emperor of the new German Empire in 1871, following France's humiliating defeat in the Franco-Prussian War. It was fitting to Clemenceau that the French should humiliate the Germans and reassert their power by signing the Treaty of Versailles in the same symbolic locale.

In the 1920s and 1930s, a cosmopolitan spirit flourished in Paris as many American and European artists, writers, and musicians moved to the city, creating an avant-garde culture. American expatriate Gertrude Stein lived in Paris at this time and coined the term “lost generation” to describe her peers. Many of these expatriates frequented the bars and restaurants in Montmartre and Montparnasse. A group of American and European artists and performers in Paris, including Man Ray, Mina Loy, Tristan Tzara, Jean Cocteau, Ezra Pound, Jane Heap, Kiki, and Martha Dennison, pose for this 1920s portrait.

Pictured here in the early 1920s is a wine store on rue des Rosiers, the Jewish Quarter in the 4th Arrondissement in the Marais. In the 1400s, Jews were expelled from the city of Paris, and they settled in the Marais, which was not a part of Paris at the time. Most of the Jews living here during Nazi occupation in World War II were sent to Nazi extermination camps. Today, rue des Rosiers is the center of the Orthodox Jewish community of Paris, and has experienced over the past half a century the immigration of Middle Eastern and North African Jews.

The Moulin Rouge with its famous red windmill, pictured here in 1925, showcased many well-known performers over its century-plus history, including Edith Piaf, Josephine Baker, and Frank Sinatra. Toulouse-Lautrec captured many bawdy scenes of the Moulin Rouge in his Post-Impressionist paintings. The historic cabaret inspired a book of the same name by Pierre la Mure, which was adapted into a movie in 1952 starring Zsa-Zsa Gabor, and another in 2001 starring Nicole Kidman.

The Louvre, shown here in 1926, was built in the late twelfth century under Philippe Auguste as a defensive fortress along the Seine. In its early days, it contained the state archives and royal treasury. Charles V, also known as Charles the Wise, turned the fortress into his royal palace in the fourteenth century, and constructed a library. Francis I updated the Louvre in Renaissance style in 1546, having architect Pierre Lescot destroy the majority of the existing structure and build a new palace on the original structure of the medieval fortress. The Louvre gained many additions over the years, including the Tuileries Palace, built by Catherine de' Medici and later connected to the Louvre. The Louvre fell into a state of abandon after the royal court moved to Versailles in 1682, and razing it was contemplated, but it was once again used by the royal family when they returned there on October 6, 1789, after the Women's March on Versailles two days earlier.

Nicola Sacco and Bartolomeo Vanzetti were Italian-American anarchists who were convicted in the United States on charges of robbery and murder, and later executed, in 1927. Their guilt was contested, many viewing them as scapegoats during the red scare in the interwar period. Their trial caused an international outcry, and millions worldwide protested their innocence, as shown here in this Communist protest in favor of Sacco and Vanzetti in Paris in 1926. Their guilt or innocence has never been proved conclusively; the evidence suggests that they supported Luigi Galleani, an Italian anarchist who advocated revolutionary violence.

Parisians in the 1920s are buying fresh vegetables at an open-air market on rue Mouffetard in the 5th Arrondissement in the Latin Quarter on the Left Bank. One of the oldest streets in Paris, rue Mouffetard was once an ancient Roman road connecting Paris to Southern Italy, via Lyon. Luckily, the area escaped destruction during Haussmann's renovations in the mid nineteenth century. Today, the street is lined with buildings dating mostly from the seventeenth century, and is a lively street of bars, cafes, restaurants, crepe stands, boutiques, open-air produce markets, and other gourmet food shops. At the southern end of rue Mouffetard is the Church of St. Medard. On the northern end is Place de la Contrescarpe, a former nineteenth-century military encampment. Hemingway lived on rue Cardinal Lemoine, a nearby street, in the 1920s, where he wrote *A Moveable Feast* about his time in Paris. Blocks away, on rue du Cardinal-Lemoine, a preserved piece of the medieval wall of Paris from the time of Philippe Auguste in the twelfth century is often overlooked by passers-by who are unaware of its historical significance.

The arrival in Paris of the American aviator Charles Lindbergh is pictured here at le Bourget after he flew the first solo non-stop transatlantic flight from New York to Paris on May 21, 1927, in his single-engine airplane *Spirit of St. Louis.* Lindbergh, nicknamed "the Lone Eagle" and "Lucky Lindy," was welcomed in Paris with an elaborate celebration in his honor after his 33.5-hour journey and presented with the Legion of Honor medal by the French president Gaston Doumerge.

Josephine Baker, the American-born French cultural icon, known as the "Black Venus" or the "Black Pearl," is shown here in the 1920s. As a child, Baker was a street performer and vaudeville chorus singer in St. Louis and New York City. When she went to Paris in 1925, she loved it so much she declared herself a citizen of France. Baker became hugely popular for her famous act, which she performed at the Folies Bergère wearing only a banana skirt and high heels, along with Chiquita, her pet cheetah. Baker enjoyed a level of success in France not possible in America in the days of segregation. She inspired the works of contemporary artists and writers like Pablo Picasso, Ernest Hemingway, and F. Scott Fitzgerald. Baker was also a social activist. She joined the Resistance and worked as a spy during World War II, and fought for the civil rights movement in America afterward. When she died at the age of 62, more than 20,000 people attended her funeral to pay their respects, during which time she was given French military honors, the first American-born woman to receive such a tribute.

The Interwar Crisis

(1930s)

People gaze at artwork on display at a stand in Montmartre in the early 1930s. At a height of more than 432 feet, Montmartre in the 18th Arrondissement is the highest point in Paris, crowned with the white dome of Sacre-Coeur at the summit. Frequented for more than a century by artists and Bohemians, such as Picasso, Dali, Monet, and Renoir, Montmartre retains a quaint village-like feel even today. Historians believe the area to have been a Druid holy site in pre-historic Paris. At the end of the nineteenth century, Montmartre became a hub of entertainment, nightclubs, cabarets, and brothels, which contributed to Paris' reputation as a city of entertainment and sin.

This postcard from 1930 depicts Sacré-Coeur, the "Basilica of the Sacred Heart," at the summit of Montmartre. The Roman Catholic Basilica was conceived after the French defeat in the Franco-Prussian War of 1870 as a tribute to the nearly 60,000 French who died in the war. The basilica was modeled from the winning design of architect Paul Abadie in a contest of more than 77 other architects in 1873. The basilica was not completed until 1914 and not consecrated until after World War I. The Roman-Byzantine-style church is built of travertine, quarried from the Château-Landon region of France, a stone special for releasing calcite, which makes it white and resists the tarnishing forces of weather and pollution. Its mosaic *Christ in Majesty* is one of the largest mosaics in the world. Sacré-Coeur has been featured in many films, such as *Sabrina* with Audrey Hepburn, and *Amélie.*

Pictured in this 1930 photograph is Place de la République, dating from the time of Haussmann. The statue of the Republic in the center by the artist Dalou dates from the 1880s and tells of the history of the French Republic.

Pictured here in 1934 is American actor Buster Keaton, at far-right, during the filming of his movie *Le Roi des Champs-Elysées (The King of the Champs-Elysées).* In the film, directed by Max Nosseck, Keaton plays both an American gangster and an aspiring actor. Keaton's part is dubbed in French, and the film was never released in the United States.

Two men spend the afternoon fishing on the banks of the Seine in 1935. For centuries, the Seine has been central to life in Paris, supporting commerce and providing recreation for Parisians and visitors. The Seine separates the two distinct sections of Paris—the Right Bank on the north side of the river and the Left Bank on the south. Most of the great monuments, museums, and important buildings in Paris are located close to the Seine. Today, commercial barges transport goods to Paris and other towns in the northwestern part of France. *Bateaux mouches* provide leisurely sightseeing cruises along the Seine for visitors.

Pigeons fly around in the square in front of Hôtel-de-Ville in the 4th Arrondissement in 1935.

Women push baby carriages in 1935 at Jardin des Plantes, a botanical garden in the 5th Arrondissement, housing Paris' natural history museum and a menagerie, one of the oldest in Europe. Built in 1626 as a medicinal herb garden for Louis XIII, the gardens were originally called Les Jardins du Roi, the King's Gardens, but they were opened to the public in 1640. During the Prussian siege of Paris in 1870, food supplies were cut off from the city, leaving Parisians no choice but to resort to eating animals from the menagerie at Jardin des Plantes, including the prized elephants, Pollux and Castor.

In preparation for the International Exposition of 1937, Exposition Internationale des Arts et Techniques dans la vie Moderne (an exposition dedicated to art and technology in modern life), the old Trocadéro Palace was demolished and the new Palais de Chaillot eventually took its place. Today, this palace houses a theater, the Naval Museum, and the Museum of Man.

This image was recorded on Bastille Day, July 14, 1935, the French national holiday that commemorates the anniversary of the storming of the Bastille on July 14, 1789, which symbolized the birth of modern France. Bastille Day celebrations in Paris include lavish parties, fireworks, and dancing. There is a huge military parade down the Champs-Elysées, which includes the French Republican Guards, the Paris Fire Brigade, and sometimes France's allies. During the parade, the French air force, the Patrouille de France, flies above, and the French president makes a speech.

During a Bastille Day rally at Place de la Bastille on July 14, 1935, the Popular Front demonstrated with a sign proclaiming their manifesto: to disarm fascist leagues, to defend and develop democratic freedoms, and to ensure human peace. The Popular Front served as the French government for only two years, from 1936 to 1938, during the volatile political and social climate of Paris in the 1930s.

Crowds climb the steps of the Pantheon on the 50th anniversary of the death of Victor Hugo in 1935. Hugo (1802–1885), the French novelist, poet, romantic playwright, and champion of human rights and Republicanism, is a French literary icon and national hero. Hugely influential in the Romantic movement, he is still seen as one of France's greatest poets. Hugo's most famous works are *Les Misérables* and *Notre-Dame de Paris (The Hunchback of Notre Dame).*

Coco Chanel (1883–1971), French *couturière,* shown here in August 1937, was one of the most important fashion designers of the twentieth century. Her designs were renowned for their elegance, simplicity, and comfort. In 1921, Chanel introduced her signature perfume, Chanel No. 5, the first internationally sold fragrance, and the favorite of Marilyn Monroe. She popularized the elegant women's skirt suit and the indispensable little black dress, an essential of haute couture. She opened a fashion boutique at 31 rue Cambron in Paris in 1918 and lived at the Ritz Hotel in Paris for 30 years, even during the Nazi occupation, at which time she had an affair with German officer Hans Gunther von Dincklage. Chanel's Nazi consorting was covered up after the war and *Time* magazine named her one of the most influential people of the twentieth century. The House of Chanel is still one of the leading Paris design houses today.

Work is under way in 1937 for the International Exposition and the demolition of the old Trocadéro Palace.

French cancan dancers are seen performing at the music hall Tabarin in 1937. The cancan dance dates back to the 1830s to the working-class dance venues of Montparnasse. Cancan, which means "tittle-tattle" or "scandal" because it was a controversial dance in its time, was also known as *chahut,* meaning "uproar" or "noise." In the nineteenth century, it was danced by a single entertainer, but developed into a chorus line performance lasting ten or more minutes. The famous elaborate dance was characterized by the *battement* (high kick), the *rond de jambe* (rapid movement of the lower leg, raised leg, long skirts held high), *port d'armes* (one leg held by the ankle and stretched vertically in the air while standing on the other), and screaming. It was immortalized on canvas in the paintings and posters of Toulouse-Lautrec, Georges Seurat, and Pablo Picasso.

A Peugeot, model 302, is displayed in Bois de Boulogne on June 5, 1937. The French car company, which has its headquarters in Paris on Avenue de la Grande Armée, is second only to Germany's Volkswagen as Europe's largest auto manufacturer. In the nineteenth century, Peugeot made bicycles. During World War II, Germany took over the Peugeot factory and used it for war production of vans and trucks, but it was heavily bombed by the Allies.

Pictured here in 1938, a boy stands beside a Wallace Fountain. A British philanthropist and Francophile, Sir Richard Wallace donated more than 50 fountains to the city of Paris after the destruction of many aqueducts during the Franco-Prussian War. Clean water was expensive, and the beautiful green drinking fountains both beautified Paris and provided free clean drinking water to anyone who wanted it. Thanks to Wallace, the urban poor had a clean and free source of water, which in theory allowed them to avoid the temptation of alcohol, alcoholism being a significant problem among the urban poor in the nineteenth century. Thirty-six additional Wallace-style fountains were later added.

Shakespeare and Company, the famous English-language bookstore, is pictured at its original location at 12 rue l'Odéon. Sylvia Beach owned the store from 1919 to 1941, and it became a hub of literary culture for the Lost Generation and a meeting spot for authors like F. Scott Fitzgerald, Gertrude Stein, Ezra Pound, James Joyce, and Ernest Hemingway. It was also a place to seek out forbidden literature, such as D. H. Lawrence's contentious *Lady Chatterly's Lover* and James Joyce's *Ulysses,* published by Beach in 1922 but banned in the United States and Great Britain. The store closed during German occupation in December 1941, but was reopened in 1951 by the American George Whitman at its new and present-day location at 37 rue de la Bûcherie across from Notre Dame on the Left Bank. Under Whitman's management, it became a center for the beat movement in Europe. Whitman, who called the bookstore a "socialist utopia," allowed people to sleep there.

Wine barrels are being unloaded in 1938 along the quais of the Seine for a Paris wine market. Winemaking in France dates back to Gallo-Roman times when the Romans spread winemaking techniques throughout Europe. Early French wines were used for both sacramental purposes and personal use. Winemaking in France thrived with Charlemagne's efforts to spread Christianity throughout the Holy Roman Empire, because the Church used a lot of wine. Up until 1650, when some French wines were first bottled and corked, French wine was sold out of casks with little identification of its origin or quality. The twentieth century brought improvements in regulating French wine production, and on July 30, 1935, with the approval of the Wine Statute, the first formal system of Appellation Control was created in France to clearly identify the origin, date, and quality of wines. Today, winemaking remains one of France's largest industries and France is the largest producer of fine wines in the world. Wines are so abundant in France at every price level that they are enjoyed by nearly all Parisians regardless of social standing.

Roger-Viollet photographic agency, at 6 rue de Seine, pictured here in May 1939, archives the majority of the historic photos displayed in this book. Henri Roger took his first photograph in Paris on October 13, 1889, and Roger-Viollet, the company founded in 1938 by his daughter Helen Fischer, has since become one of the world's three greatest photographic agencies, and the one with the most extensive historic photo archives of Paris, largely as a result of acquiring large collections from great photographers around the world. In 1994, the last will of Helen Fischer and her husband, Jean Fischer, transferred their property and photographic collections to ownership by the city of Paris.

Riders in the 33rd Tour de France cycling race ride on the Champs-Elysées through the Arc de Triomphe on the final day of the race on July 30, 1939, as throngs of excited fans watch. The race that year was significant because it occurred on the eve of World War II. Given all the tension in Europe at the time, Italy, Germany, and Spain decided not to participate, so the 1938 winner of the race, Italian Gino Bartali, was not allowed to defend his title. The 1939 race was the last Tour to be held for eight years until it resumed after the war in 1947. The first Tour de France started in 1903 as an event to endorse the newspaper *L'auto,* now called *L'Équipe* by Henri Desgrange, the editor. The Tour is a three-week bicycle race held in stages, consisting of 20-22 teams, and composed of 9 riders to a team. Each stage is a race over the course of a day, with around 20 stages, for a total of 1,800 to nearly 2,500 miles. A rider's time for each stage is counted and added. Since 1975, the Tour de France, the most famous cycling race in the world, has ended on the Champs-Elysées, and riders know they are near the finish line when the Arc de Triomphe comes into view. Lance Armstrong won the race seven straight times between 1999 and 2005.

Pablo Picasso poses in his Paris studio in 1939. Behind him on the right is an example of his art. Picasso spent a great deal of time in Paris between 1901 and his death in 1973, especially in the Montmartre and Montparnasse districts. Among his circle of friends were Andre Breton, Guillaume Apollinaire, and Gertrude Stein.

A classic Parisian brasserie, such as the one shown here in 1939, is a combination of cafe and restaurant. Dining is an important part of French life. In Paris, where high-quality food is available all year round, cooking is an art form. French chefs are celebrities—the most renowned and skilled of them are rewarded the Legion of Honor. Parisian culinary passion is reflected in the number of places to dine in the city—well in excess of 20,000. Paris became known for its gastronomic diversity of foods after the introduction of railways, when droves of migrants from all over France flocked to Paris, bringing with them their favorite regional recipes. Today, because of the vast variety of people of different cultures living in Paris, Parisians and visitors to the city can enjoy the finest French cuisine, as well as food from all over the world.

This photograph of a Paris cafe was taken in 1940. Cafes are an integral part of Parisian life, where people network, socialize, do business, and observe the world around them for hours. Many cafes have indoor as well as outdoor seating, and most have full menus. Some of the most famous Parisian cafes are Les Deux Magots, Café de Flore, and Café de la Paix.

Café Procope, pictured here on rue de l'Ancienne Comédie in the 6th Arrondissement, opened in 1686 and is the oldest existing cafe in Paris. In the eighteenth century, it was a meeting spot for the Philosophes, like Voltaire, Diderot, and Rousseau, and later for French Revolutionaries Robespierre, Danton, and Marat. Its other notable patrons included Thomas Jefferson, Benjamin Franklin, and Napoleon Bonaparte. They discussed philosophy and politics over coffee and hot chocolate, which at that time were highly exotic items from the new world and West Indies. Today, Le Procope is a restaurant.

German soldiers look on curiously at the Tomb of the Unknown Soldier as they march under the Arc de Triomphe shortly after the start of their Occupation in Paris in 1940. After six weeks of fighting, and French losses of 130,000 people, France surrendered on June 24, 1940. Two-thirds of France became occupied and controlled by the Nazis. The Allies had suffered a crushing defeat in the Battle of France and signed an armistice on June 22, in Compiègne, France. The armistice was advantageous for Hitler because it removed further military threats from French forces fighting from North Africa, and from the French Navy, and installed a French government of sorts, creating a sense of normalcy. Leaving a French government intact also spared Germany the encumbrance of administering French territories and allowed Hitler to focus on Great Britain, where he anticipated another swift conquest.

The War Years—Occupation and Liberation

(1940–1945)

During the Occupation, German troops infiltrated every quarter in the city—shown clearly in this 1940 photograph of German soldiers marching down the steps at Sacré-Coeur on Montmartre. A growing number of French who strongly opposed the far left in France preferred a fascist regime and even German occupation to a government ruled by communists and socialists.

In early 1940, with the advent of German occupation, the French severed the elevator cable on the Eiffel Tower so that the Germans and Hitler, if he came to visit, would have to climb the tower to reach the top. Later in 1940, Adolf Hitler stands in front of the Eiffel Tower with a group of his trusted advisors, among them Speer and Giesler, inspecting his latest conquest and contemplating his enormous European power. On this trip, Hitler declined to climb the Eiffel Tower steps; German soldiers did arrive at the top, climbing approximately 80 stories to raise their swastika flag. Hitler is said to have spent hours at the tomb of Napoleon at Les Invalides. It is intriguing to speculate on what Hitler may have been thinking as he gazed on the tomb of Napoleon, the man who, like Hitler, had conquered much of Europe, but eventually lost everything. Hitler never returned to Paris.

German soldiers push their bicycles at Place de la Concorde on July 19, 1941. During the Occupation, the Germans allowed only 700 motor vehicle permits in Paris, and private cars were banned and replaced with horse-drawn carriages and two million bicycles. By the end of World War II, new bicycles in Paris were at such a premium, they cost nearly as much as prewar cars.

Flags of Nazi Germany are displayed on rue de Rivoli on the facade of Hôtel Meurice, where German military authorities lived during the Occupation.

This statue of the Marquis du Condorcet (1847–1915), a French political figure, is being destroyed and melted down for scrap metal by the Nazis in 1941. Hundreds of statues in Paris met the same fate during the war.

Young *pétainistes,* supporters of Pétain, are pictured here on May 1, 1941. On July 10, 1940, French representatives of the National Assembly had voted vast judicial, administrative, executive, and diplomatic powers to Pétain. The legality of this has been debated by the French government and French historians owing to disregard for legal proceedings, the use of threat and intimidation, bribes, and the absence of 27 key representatives who were on board the ship *Massilia* going to North Africa. It was also in violation of an 1884 constitutional amendment forbidding giving power to a non-Republican regime. Under these dubious conditions of the vote, Pétain was now the "head of the French state." Pétain also had the power to appoint his successor. He named Pierre Laval as his vice-president and future successor. Pétain was supported by paramilitary fascist groups, like the French Legion of Fighters, L.C.F., which helped the Nazis, and other supporting groups.

Onlookers curiously study the "head of a Jew," modeled as some pseudo-scientific oddity with exaggerated racial features at the anti-Jewish Exposition in the Palace Berlitz, 1941. The exhibition was put on by the Nazis to incite anti-Semitism against French Jews, and met with no public outcry. More than 200,000 visitors came to see the exhibit. During the German occupation, Jews in France, like those in other European countries, had to wear yellow badges identifying themselves as Jews. In October 1940, Jews were forbidden from working in administration, arts, media, entertainment, or from being teachers, doctors, or lawyers. Jewish homes were subject to random raids, their phones were confiscated, and an early curfew was enforced. Jews could not gather in public places, and could only sit in the last car of the Metro.

Pictured here in 1944, Parisians line up to buy vegetables and other food items—a common sight during the Occupation. Paris was under severe rationing during the war, and people exchanged food stamps for food, waiting in line for hours for their rations. The severe rationing affected city youth especially. During this time, coffee was replaced with chicory, or even worse, a repulsive blend of acorns and chickpeas called "cafe national." Long periods went by when there was no meat available. Parisians even raised rabbits in their apartments for food. After 1943, conditions became far worse, and Parisians were rationed to 1,000 calories a day.

Women in the French militia are shown distributing bottles of wine to German soldiers in April 1944. During the Occupation, most Parisians kept to themselves and silently endured. Others exploited, and even profited from opportunities in the black market created by the war. Although there were severe rationings during the war, coveted items that were unavailable to the general public, like wine and cigarettes, could often be bought at exorbitant rates. Many French tried to ingratiate themselves to their German occupiers by providing them with prohibited luxury items, although they would be severely punished after the war for consorting with the enemy.

American infantry march past the Arc de Triomphe during the liberation of Paris on the Champs-Elysées.

German soldiers are taken prisoner at the Place de l'Opéra during the liberation of Paris on August 25, 1944.

Parisians take to the streets to celebrate the end of the Occupation. Parisians and Allied troops show off a captured Nazi flag in front of Opéra Garnier.

Exuberant Parisian women rush to welcome their American saviors on the Champs-Elysées during the liberation of Paris. In 1944, Frenchwomen also received the right to vote for the first time.

Parisians and Allied soldiers hold a portrait of Hitler upside down to demonstrate victory during the Liberation.

American soldiers stand in front of Notre Dame during the Liberation, the site of much celebration. Unlike most other European cities during the war, Paris emerged mostly unscathed. This was partly owing to its few targets of military importance, but it is mostly owing to the decisions of one man. When it was clear that Germany was going to be overpowered by the Allies, Hitler ordered the German military governor of Paris, General Dietrich von Choltitz, to destroy Paris before the German withdrawal. Fortunately for the world, von Choltitz disobeyed orders, deciding that he would rather be remembered as the man who saved Paris, not the man responsible for its destruction. Choltitz and 17,000 of his troops surrendered to Allied forces and the Resistance at Gare Montparnasse upon the liberation of Paris on August 25, 1944.

German prisoners of war are being led away after the liberation of Paris in August 1944. Liberation in France was followed by a series of executions, and *éputation sauvage*—wild civil justice without legal proceedings. French people who collaborated with the Nazis in any way or who participated in the black market were shamed as war profiteers. Others who took advantage of wartime desperation by price gouging were called "BOF" for *beurre, oeuf, fromage*—meaning butter, eggs, and cheese. Thousands of Frenchwomen who served as prostitutes for the Nazis or consorted with them had their heads publicly shaved or were otherwise humiliated. Once a provisional French government reestablished order, collaborators were put on trial according to legal procedure.

German prisoners of war are being marched through Luxembourg Gardens after the liberation of Paris on August 25, 1944. Pierre Laval was executed after trial for treason on October 4, 1945. Philippe Pétain was charged with treason and sentenced to death by firing squad, but Charles de Gaulle reduced his sentence to life imprisonment. Maurice Papon was amnestied and resumed his position in the police. He would later be responsible for the Paris Massacre of 1961 and was finally convicted for crimes against humanity in 1998. He served only 3 years in prison before he died in 2007. Numerous criminals of war were not tried until the 1980s. Some collaborators participated in terrorist movements during the Algerian War for Independence.

A lone American soldier wanders through the Hall of Mirrors at Versailles in 1944 after the liberation of Paris.

Micheline Francey, a popular French actress in the late 1940s and early 1950s, descends a flight of stairs on the Right Bank, against the backdrop of the Eiffel Tower. Among her most successful films were *Raspoutine, Passion De Femmes, La Fete a Henriette,* and *Rita.*

Les Invalides is a group of buildings in the 7th Arrondissement on the Left Bank near the Eiffel Tower, including a French military museum, monuments, tombs for French war heroes, and a retirement home and hospital for war veterans. Invalides began as a project of Louis XIV in 1670 to create a residence and hospital for sick and aged soldiers in what was then the suburbs of Paris. The Hôpital des Invalides was completed by French architect Libéral Bruant in 1676, and a chapel for the veterans added in 1679 called Église Saint-Louis des Invalides. Louis XIV had a royal private chapel separately added, the Église of the Dôme, the most identifiable feature of Les Invalides, in 1708. The Dôme church was modeled on St. Peter's Basilica in Rome. The interior of this church was painted by Charles de la Fosse, the disciple of French painter Le Brun. Les Invalides is the final resting place of Emperor Napoleon Bonaparte, whose remains were transferred here to an elaborate crypt under the dome in 1861. Also buried at Invalides are Napoleon's brothers, his son, some of his military officers, and other military heroes.

Sainte-Chapelle and the Palace of Justice in the 1st Arrondissement on Île de la Cité, shown here in September 1949, was built on the site of the Royal Palace of Louis IX, canonized as Saint Louis. During Haussmann's rebuilding of Paris, the Palace of Justice was built around the medieval cathedral, virtually imprisoning it, as evidenced in this image. The complex of buildings now contains various French courts, and the Conciergerie, the former prison.

The Postwar Years

(1946–1950s)

Sainte-Chapelle is a Gothic masterpiece that leaves a lasting impression on all who visit, because of its stained-glass windows, considered to be the most beautiful in the world. The transposing jewel colors from the stained glass illuminate the entire chapel. Sainte-Chapelle was built under the rule of Louis IX, known as Louis the Blessed, to house the Crown of Thorns, the holy relic the king acquired in Venice via Constantinople in 1239. Architect Pierre de Montreuil, also known for Saint Germain des Pres, designed this exquisite architectural marvel, consecrated on Île de la Cité in 1248. Sainte-Chapelle has two chapels. The upper chapel, which houses the reliquary surrounded by exquisite jewels, was once reserved for the royal family. Fifteen massive windows from the thirteenth century display more than 1,100 biblical and evangelical scenes spanning 6,650 square feet.

Polish visitors pay homage at the grave of Polish-born piano composer Fréderic Chopin, on the centennial anniversary of his death, at Père-Lachaise cemetery in November 1949. Considered to be a child prodigy, Chopin moved to Paris at age 20 where he composed, performed, and taught music. Between 1837 and 1847, Chopin had an affair in Paris with French writer George Sand (also known as Aurore Dudevant). Chopin's close friend, artist Delacroix, painted Chopin and George Sand. Chopin died at the age of 39 of tuberculosis, and is still regarded as one of the finest pianists and composers in history.

General Dwight D. Eisenhower stands at the Arc de Triomphe on November 11, 1951. As Supreme Commander of the Allied Expeditionary Forces in Europe during World War II, he had been instrumental in the D-Day invasion and liberation of France. Eisenhower was elected President of the United States the year after this photograph was taken, serving for two terms.

Workers clean the lamps on Pont Alexandre III, shown here in June 1956. Pont Alexandre III, Paris' most beautiful bridge, traverses the Seine, connecting Les Invalides on the Left Bank to the Champs-Elysées quarter on the Right Bank. It was a gift from the Russian Tsar, Nicholas II, and named for his father, Tsar Alexandre III, as a tribute to the Franco-Russian Dual Alliance, formed against an aggressive Germany in 1892. Construction of the bridge by French engineers Alby and Résal started in 1896 and finished in time for the Exposition Universelle of 1900. The bridge is a wonder of Belle Époque engineering, with a 6-meter-high, single span arch of steel, the first of its kind in Paris. Its majestic Art Nouveau style, with gold-plated bronze statues, nymphs, cherubs, and flying horses atop 17-meter columns symbolizing "Rénommées" near Pegasus, complements the Grand and Petit Palais behind it on the Right Bank.

NOTES ON THE PHOTOGRAPHS

These notes, listed by page number, attempt to include all aspects known of the photographs. Each of the photographs is identified by the page number, a title or description, photographer and collection, archive, and call or box number when applicable. Although every attempt was made to collect all data, in some cases complete data may have been unavailable due to the age and condition of some of the photographs and records.

ii **LIBERATION**
Library of Congress
LC-USW36-1

vi **GRAND POND**
The Roger–Viollet Agency
RV 3215-16

x **PARIS PANORAMA**
The Roger–Viollet Agency
RV 13746-6

2 **STROLLING IN THE RAIN**
The Roger–Viollet Agency
RV 12448-24

3 **ARC DE TRIOMPHE**
Library of Congress
LC-USZ62-63736

4 **PONT DE ARTS**
The Roger–Viollet Agency
RV 1502-12

5 **ST. JACQUES TOWER**
Library of Congress
LC-USZ62-1109108

6 **PLACE DU CHÂTELET**
Library of Congress
LC-USZ62-110907

7 **PLACE ST. GERMAIN L'AUXERROIS**
Library of Congress
LC-USZ62-110911

8 **PALAIS DES THERMES**
Library of Congress
LC-USZ62-110903

9 **DISASTER**
The Roger–Viollet Agency
RV 9131-816

10 **BOULEVARD ST. DENIS**
Library of Congress
LC-USZ62-123749

11 **LIBERTY HEAD**
Library of Congress
LC-USZ62-18086

12 **HÔTEL DE VILLE**
Library of Congress
LC-USZ62-128604

13 **ART STUDENTS**
Library of Congress
LC-DIG-ppmsc-04833

14 **EIFFEL TOWER**
The Roger–Viollet Agency
RV 1081-13

15 **GUSTAVE EIFFEL**
Library of Congress
LC-USZ62-24985

16 **HYDRAULIC MACHINERY**
Library of Congress
LC-USZ62-11264

17 **VENETIAN GLASSMAKING**
The Roger–Viollet Agency
RV 12126-1

18 **GAS PAVILION**
Library of Congress
LC-USZ62-102670

19 **GALLERY OF MACHINES**
Library of Congress
LC-USZ62-101104

20 **ORNATE FOOTBRIDGE**
Library of Congress
LC-USZ62-102647

21 **THE FIGARO IN ICE**
The Roger–Viollet Agency
RV 3316-9

22 **PALACE OF JUSTICE**
Library of Congress
LC-USZ62-117044

23 **THE PANTHEON**
Library of Congress
LC-DIG-ppmsc-05171

24 **GARE DU NORD**
Library of Congress
LC-USZ62-133257

26 **LUXEMBOURG GARDENS**
The Roger–Viollet Agency
RV 13908-4

27 **TRAIN ACCIDENT**
The Roger–Viollet Agency
RV 5042-4

28 **AUGUSTE RODIN**
Library of Congress
LC-USZ62-102764

29 **EMILE ZOLA**
The Roger–Viollet Agency
RV 1296-15

30 **MOULIN ROUGE**
The Roger–Viollet Agency
RV 2575-10

31 **ROMAN ART**
The Roger–Viollet Agency
RV 23032-7

32 **GARE D'ORSAY**
The Roger–Viollet Agency
RV 23417-148

33 **WEDDING DAY**
The Roger–Viollet Agency
RV 21676-1

34 **SOCIETY FOR ANIMAL RELIEF**
Library of Congress
LC-DIG-ggbain-00556

35 **PLACE DES VOSGES**
The Roger–Viollet Agency
RV 24684-18

36 **EIFFEL TOWER**
Library of Congress
LC-USZ62-94920

37 **Steam Omnibus**
Library of Congress
LC-USZ62-45066

38 **Flower Wagon**
The Roger–Viollet Agency
RV 13717-7

39 **Notre Dame**
Library of Congress
LC-USZ62-63738

40 **Notre Dame no. 2**
Library of Congress
LC-USZ62-69838

41 **Harry Houdini**
Library of Congress
LC-USZ62-112430

42 **Gallery d'Apollon**
Library of Congress
LC-USZ62-63742

43 **Avenue du Bois**
Library of Congress
LC-USZ62-63743

44 **Place de la Concorde**
Library of Congress
LC-USZ62-123716

45 **Metro Construction**
The Roger–Viollet Agency
RV 722-6

46 **Making Dresses**
The Roger–Viollet Agency
RV 1045-12

47 **Diplodocus**
The Roger–Viollet Agency
RV 20247-1

48 **Eiffel Tower**
Library of Congress
LC-USZ62-107932

49 **Massive Pumpkins**
The Roger–Viollet Agency
RV 985-12

50 **Opera Garnier**
Library of Congress
LC-USZ62-63746

51 **Opera Exterior**
Library of Congress
LC-USZ62-106358

52 **Paris Flood, 1910**
The Roger–Viollet Agency
RV 13343-3

53 **Paris Flood no. 2**
The Roger–Viollet Agency
RV 3893-10

54 **La Madeleine**
Library of Congress
LC-USZ6-1900

55 **Street Salesmen**
The Roger–Viollet Agency
RV 722-4

56 **Paris Metro Entrance**
The Roger–Viollet Agency
RV 915-6

57 **French Reservists**
Library of Congress
LC-DIG-ggbain-16970

58 **Off to War**
Library of Congress
LC-DIG-ggbain-16958

59 **Colonial Troops**
The Roger–Viollet Agency
RV 1616-4

60 **Signing Up**
The Roger–Viollet Agency
RV 2362-2

61 **Injured Veteran**
The Roger–Viollet Agency
RV 912-7

62 **French Regiment**
The Roger–Viollet Agency
RV 484-9

64 **Young Soldiers**
The Roger–Viollet Agency
RV 836-6

65 **The Enemy Is Listening**
The Roger–Viollet Agency
RV 836-10

66 **Unexploded Zeppelin**
The Roger–Viollet Agency
RV 444-4

67 **French Children**
Library of Congress
LC-USZ62-98319

68 **Repairing Carpets**
The Roger–Viollet Agency
RV 1067-9

69 **Three Leaders**
The Roger–Viollet Agency
RV 601-10

70 **Hall of Mirrors**
The Roger–Viollet Agency
RV 973-5

71 **Lost Generation**
Library of Congress
LC-USZ62-113902

72 **Wine Store**
The Roger–Viollet Agency
RV 1970-3

73 **Moulin Rouge**
The Roger–Viollet Agency
RV 1876-11

74 **The Louvre**
Library of Congress
LC-USZ62-46723

75 **Communist Protest**
The Roger–Viollet Agency
RV 10211-2

76 **Open-air Market**
The Roger–Viollet Agency
RV 10207-5

77 **Lindbergh Arrives**
The Roger–Viollet Agency
RV 1267-9

78 **Josephine Baker**
The Roger–Viollet Agency
RV 13273-1

80 **Street Artwork**
The Roger–Viollet Agency
RV 10148-1

81 **Sacré-Coeur**
The Roger–Viollet Agency
RV 25523-2

82 **The Republic**
The Roger–Viollet Agency
RV 11009-14

83 **Buster Keaton**
The Roger–Viollet Agency
RV 12125-11

84 **Men Fishing**
The Roger–Viollet Agency
RV 14139

85 **Pigeons Flying**
The Roger–Viollet Agency
RV 11169-2

86 **Woman on a Stroll**
The Roger–Viollet Agency
RV 13525-2

87 **Preparing for Exposition**
The Roger–Viollet Agency
RV 5217-13

88 **Bastille Day**
The Roger–Viollet Agency
RV 12077-1

89 **The Popular Front**
The Roger–Viollet Agency
RV 1355-2

90 **The Pantheon**
The Roger–Viollet Agency
RV 13739-10

91 **Coco Chanel**
The Roger–Viollet Agency
RV 10466-4

92 **International Expo**
The Roger–Viollet Agency
RV 4268-2

93 **Cancan Dancers**
The Roger–Viollet Agency
RV 8921-13

94 **Peugeot**
The Roger–Viollet Agency
RV 1330-2

95 **Wallace Fountain**
The Roger–Viollet Agency
RV 1097-15

96 **Shakespeare and Company**
The Roger–Viollet Agency
RV 2098-7

97 **Unloading Barrels**
The Roger–Viollet Agency
RV 3306-2

98 **Roger-Viollet Agency**
The Roger–Viollet Agency
RV 17965-4

99 **33rd Tour de France**
The Roger–Viollet Agency
RV 1207-6

100 **Pablo Picasso**
Library of Congress
LC-USZ62-99813

101 **Brasserie**
Library of Congress
LC-USZ62-95976

102 **Paris Cafe**
The Roger–Viollet Agency
RV 1193-10

103 **Cafe Procope**
The Roger–Viollet Agency
RV 4180-22

104 **Tomb of the Unknown Soldier**
The Roger–Viollet Agency
RV 533-2

106 **German Troops**
The Roger–Viollet Agency
RV 1197-7

107 **Hitler**
Library of Congress
LC-USZ62-50036

108 **German Bicycles**
The Roger–Viollet Agency
RV 532-10

109 **German Nazi Flags**
The Roger–Viollet Agency
RV 20133-21

110 **Marquis du Condorcet**
The Roger–Viollet Agency
RV 19463-6

111 **Young Petainistes**
The Roger–Viollet Agency
RV 19866-3

112 **Propaganda**
The Roger–Viollet Agency
RV 1085-12

113 **Ration Line**
The Roger–Viollet Agency
RV 1580-11

114 **Wine for Soldiers**
The Roger–Viollet Agency
RV 1476-6

115 **American Soldiers**
The Roger–Viollet Agency
RV 2164-8

116 **Germans Captured**
The Roger–Viollet Agency
RV 1939-1

117 **Freedom in Streets**
The Roger–Viollet Agency
RV 7998-6

118 **Frenchwomen Greeting Soldiers**
The Roger–Viollet Agency
RV 2084-13

119 **Liberation from Hitler**
The Roger–Viollet Agency
RV 12125-15

120 **Soldiers at Notre Dame**
The Roger–Viollet Agency
RV 19910-19

121 **German POWs**
The Roger–Viollet Agency
RV 2161-12

122 **Marching Prisoners**
The Roger–Viollet Agency
RV 1150-7

123 **Hall of Mirrors**
Library of Congress
LC-DIG-ppmsca-13358

124 **Micheline Francey**
The Roger–Viollet Agency
RV 14167-17

125 **Les Invalides**
The Roger–Viollet Agency
RV 25333-8

126 **Palace of Justice**
The Roger–Viollet Agency
RV 4602-15

128 **Sainte Chapelle Interior**
The Roger–Viollet Agency
RV 2473-7

129 **Polish Visitors**
The Roger–Viollet Agency
RV 14131-9

130 **Eisenhower**
The Roger–Viollet Agency
RV 13724-4

131 **Cleaning Lamps**
The Roger–Viollet Agency
RV 2518-16

Printed in the USA
CPSIA information can be obtained
at www.ICGtesting.com
JSHW072025140824
68134JS00042B/3790